T0065447

Our Wife Has Gone Mad

(A Play)

Our Wife Has Gone Mad

Our Wife Has Gone Mad
(A Play)

'Bode Ojoniyi

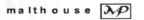

Malthouse Press Limited

Lagos, Benin, Ibadan, Jos, Port-Harcourt, Zaria

© Olabode Ojoniyi 2021
First Published 2021
ISBN: 978-978-58298-2-2

Published in Nigeria by

Malthouse Press Limited
43 Onitana Street, Off Stadium Hotel Road,
Off Western Avenue, Lagos Mainland
E-mail: malthouselagos@gmail.com
Facebook:@malthouselagos
Twitter:@malthouselagos
Istagram:@malthouselagos
Tel: 0802 600 3203

Distributors:

African Books Collective Ltd, Oxford, UK
Email: abc@africanbookscollective.com
Website: http://www.africanbookscollective.com

Foreword

When some seven years ago I wrote the Foreword to his third play, *Once Upon an Evil Genius*, I had promised readers to 'expect better days from the creative *opus* of 'Bode Ojoniyi'. I think that I have been proven right with his latest outing, *Our Wife has gone Mad*. I am aware that since the publication of *Evil Genius*, there have been six other plays in two collections.

His present play, *Our Wife has gone Mad* can be said to be a parody of two earlier plays: *Our Husband has gone Mad Again* by Ola Rotimi and *Our Wives have gone Mad Again* by Tracie Utoh-Ezeajugh. While in Rotimi's play it is the husband that runs 'mad' with political power and three wives whom he married for political expediency, the wives in Utoh-Ezeajugh change husbands at will or fight them frontally. *Our Wife* presents a more complex scenario uncommon to most, if not all, cultures of the world, much more Africa!

Daniela is the first wife of Alhaji Sule but things turn out for the worse when just three months into their marriage, Alhaji takes a second wife and thereafter a third. In a manner of 'speaking back', Daniela goes ahead to take a second and third husbands to be at par with Alhaji Sule, her first husband. This revolutionary act of Daniella is unknown to Alhaji or any of the two other husbands – all three spread across Lagos, Port Harcourt and Beijing, China. She has a boy each for the three husbands. The truth, however, is revealed when Daniela is involved in a ghastly road accident and is in a coma for sometimes. It is during this space of time that we begin to interrogate the reality or 'unreality' of her act in marrying three men at the same time. On her recovery from coma, she confronts head-on the three men to whom also she has been the bread winner for years.

In *Our Wife*, Ojoniyi takes the fight for feminist equality to the realm of the ludicrous. This is because while it is common to hear of women who are married to more than one man in a lifetime, it is *normally* after a divorce or death of the husband. In the case of Daniela, she appropriates the same liberty or privilege given to men and *marries* the men. She does not *cheat* on the first husband; she merely, legally gets married to the other two men and keeps them in their different cities, after all, some men do this too. She feels that since she has the wherewithal to take care of them as men do she is equally free to do so. She seems to enjoy a certain Lacanian superiority (indeed, a certain erotic superiority) over the men and she truly exploits it in a manner reminiscent of the 17th century writing, *Female Pre-eminence: Or the Dignity and Excellency of that Sex, above the Male* by Heinrich Cornelius Agrippa and Henry Care.

Our heroine enjoys her superiority for a good number of years and the playwright seems to have empowered her for this period only to await societal censure. But then, Ojoniyi becomes seemingly sermonizing when he makes his heroine (or is it anti-heroine?), Daniela, to turn to God at the end of the play for her 'sin' of marrying more than one husband. This is a betrayal of the feminist tradition or agenda, and core/mainstream feminists are likely to disparage him for this betrayal. I am, again, however, not sure if Ojoniyi himself set out in the first place to write a feminist play other than a castigation of same.

In all, for those who have had the opportunity of reading Ojoniyi's about a dozen plays, one thing is observable – he has grown with every outing in philosophy and depth in the delineation of character and subject matter.

Ameh Dennis Akoh, *PhD*
Professor of Drama & Critical Theory
Federal University Ndufu-Alike, Ikwo (FUNAI)

Author's Note

I chanced on the idea to write this play fortuitously. It was in the preparation for my LIT407: Modern African Drama classes. I had selected plays from leading African playwrights and the new ones for the classes. One of the themes that I wanted to explore in the plays has to do with intertextuality (writing back). Consequently, apart from plays like *The Strong Breed, No More the Wasted Breed, Death Not A Redeemer, Death and King's Horse Man, Dry Leaves on Ukan Trees,* I had equally selected *Our Husband Has Gone Mad Again* and *Our Wives Have Gone Mad Again.* In the course of my examining the intertexual relationship, the actual basis for *Our Wives Have Gone Mad Again* as a write back to *Our Husband Has Gone Mad Again,* I noticed a fundamental lacuna in their intertexual relationship. *Our Husband Has Gone Mad Again* is fundamentally built on the issue of polygamy which is not what is addressed in *Our Wives Have Gone Mad Again.* I was therefore interested in a write back that will create a polyandry. I was interested in a woman who will marry and manage at least two or three men together... So, at the 2015 Playwrights' Confab held at Kwara State University from 2 to 8 of March in Ilorin, I discussed the project at one of the workshops and there and then, Dr. Grace Adinku from University of Ghana, Legon, told me the story of this woman who actually married three men and managed the relationships until an accident occurred...Thank you Dr. Grace Adinku! Here, I present the story to the whole world from the accident as a motif for the revelations of certain secrets of the living...

I must say two things finally. First, the manuscript of this play in its unpublished form won the 2017 SONTA, Society of Nigeria Theatre Artists/Olu-Obafemi Award for playwriting. And, second, to appreciate Professor A.D. Akoh who agreed to write the foreword to this play but to suggest that we should be open to see Daniel's decision to seek the fourth man beyond mere religious reading as suggested in the foreword or in the play.

'Bode Ojoniyi

Characters

Alhaji Sule – First husband

Elder Dominion Akpan – Second husband

Chin-Chung – Third husband

Daniela – Wife

Matron Haywire

Sister Kate

Nurse 1

Nurse 2

Alhaja

Segilola

Production History

The first public reading performance of the play takes place on the 21st of January, 2017 with the following cast:

First husband: Akin Atoyebi: Alhaji Sule

Second husband: Oyewole Oyeniran, Elder Dominion Akpan

Third husband: Moses Bamidele: Chin-Chung

Wife: Temitope Ojoniyi & Adeyemo Oluwasola Glory: Daniela

Matron Haywire: Bolanle Taiwo

Sister Kate: Omolara Kemi Taiwo

Nurse 1: Taiwo Adeyemo

Nurse 2: Ibukun Bolaji Taiwo

Alhaja: Moyosola Ojoniyi

Segilola: Moyinoluwa Ojoniyi

Happenings

[*A very serene hospital reception. Three nurses are seen whispering in low tones. They cast glances at Alhaji Sule, Alhaja and Segilola. Alhaji Sule is particularly restless. He starts pacing up and down the reception. He turns to the nurses at the reception table. An argument ensues. Now, the nurses are finding it difficult to deal with Alhaji Sule. Alhaja and Segilola who have also come with Alhaji Sule to see Daniela join in the argument*].

Nurse 1:   [*Addressing Sister Kate*] Yesterday, he was here. He said the woman is his first wife. He wept and wept when he saw the woman.

Nurse 2:   But, immediately he left, another man came in. He said the same woman is his wife.

Sister Kate: *Henhen*, unbelievable! Are you sure of what you are saying?

Nurse 1:   Sure of what? We are confused!

Nurse 2:   How can we be sure of such claims? The woman is still in a coma. There is no way to confirm anything from her.

Sister Kate: This is very serious. And, the second man?

Nurse 2:	Yes, he said he flew in to Lagos from Port-Harcourt, the oil city, immediately he heard of the wife's accident!
Sister Kate:	[*Mouth opens wide in total disbelief*] The wife's accident?
Nurse 1:	He was also crying like a baby...
Nurse 2:	Rolling on the floor...
Sister Kate:	*Haba*, and what did you tell him; that another man has also claimed the woman as his wife?
Nurse 1:	We dared nothing. We were not sure of anything!
Nurse 2:	Sister, it was not a Nollywood! It was live and real!
Sister Kate:	Maybe she is a divorcee! Did you try to confirm?
Nurse 1:	Confirm, from who? The woman is still in a coma.
Nurse 2:	Ha, from the men's reactions, we could not ask such a question!
Sister Kate:	The world has gone berserk!
Nurse 1:	I cannot imagine any other thing!
	[*Alhaji Sule could not hold himself back. He confronts the Nurses*]
Alhaji Sule:	Hei, please, can somebody tell me what is happening here? I have been waiting for over an hour to see my Daniela. I have come with her

co-wives, but you have kept us waiting since, and all you do is gossip, I mean gossip while we wait endlessly, imagine such frivolities!

Sister Kate: Please, Alhaji, we are not gossips and we have no time for frivolities. We are doing our jobs. We are only trying to take the necessary precaution in the matter we have on our hands.

Alhaji Sule: There they go, what nonsensical precaution prevents you from speaking to me to inform me of the state of things with my Daniela? Tell me, what has happened to her? [*Shouting*] Please, tell me?

[*Alhaja and Segilola rush to Alhaji*]

Alhaja: Alhaji, please, what has happened?

Segilola: [*To the Nurses*]. Please, tell us what has happened to her?

Sister Kate: Nothing has happened to anybody. I understand that the patient is in a more stable condition...

Alhaji Sule: I am not here for any patient, madam. I am here for my Daniela. I want to see her...I want to see my wife, don't you understand?

Sister Kate: Alhaji, you will see your wife very shortly, but please, let me speak with the Matron. Please, a minute.

Alhaji Sule: Oh no! But you know you still have to speak with your Matron while you were here engaged in useless gossip? Oh mine, mine, the world has turned upside down!

[*Sister Kate goes into the Matron's Office to the left of the stage*]

Nurse 1: Alhaji, we are not gossips. We are only trying to take the necessary precaution on the matter.

Alhaji Sule: 'Necessary precaution' on what? My wife is on admission, I was here yesterday to see her, and I am here again to see her. My wife...I mean, my wife! So, what is the fuss over 'necessary precaution' in a man seeing his wife who is on hospital admission?

[*The Matrons rushes in. She is closely followed by Sister Kate who seems a bit confused. Matron swiftly moves to Alhaji, pleads with him and asks him to come to follow her immediately. Alhaji and his wives exit with the Matron*]

Matron: Oh Alhaji, I am very sorry for whatever has happened. I just learnt that you have been around for about an hour to see your wife. I am very sorry... but, I can assure you that she is in a very stable condition. You don't need to really worry about her. She is in capable hands.

Alhaji Sule: Good to see you Matron. I am most grateful for what you did yesterday. I know you would have treated us differently if we had met you on our arrival. At the same time, thank you.

Matron: Please, shall we go now?

Alhaji Sule: Yes, yes... Alhaja, Segi, please, let us go.

Matron: [*Leading the way*]. This way please.

[*Sister Kate is in a disbelief. She looks on at the Matron until she disappears with Alhaji and his wives. She turns to the nurses in total shock*]

Nurse 2:   Sister Kate, what happened?

Sister Kate: [*As if coming to a realization*].So strange... absolutely strange. The Matron has never been like this before! The world has gone berserk.

Nurse 1:   Tell us what happened in there?

Sister Kate: Unbelievable! The whole story is insane...

Nurse 2:   What?

Sister Kate: Immediately I mentioned that Alhaji Sule is around, before I could say any other word, Matron rose up fiercely, pushed me aside and rushed out of her office!

Nurse 1:   Is that?

Nurse 2:   Without saying a word to you?

Nurse 1:   That is indeed bizarre!

Sister Kate: A woman in coma, two men claiming to be her husband. One, Alhaji Sule...

Nurse 2:   The other, elder Dominion Akpan.

Nurse 1:   One Yoruba...

Sister Kate: The other Calabar ... an insane scenario with a wide Matron on the loose!

Nurse 2:   She has never been like that before, something must have come over her...

Nurse 1:	Like some sort of demons or gnomes from the underworld?
Sister Kate:	Hei, this is not a laughing or a joking matter! I mean it, this is strange!

[*The Matron comes in. She is still very much unsettled. She addresses the nurses*]

Matron:	Sisters, we have a very serious matter on our hands and we must manage it well. We must manage it professionally before we come to know what is true against what is not. We already have two men claiming to be the husband of the woman on admission.
Nurse 1:	Husband or husbands?
Matron:	What did I say? And which one is correct, husband or husbands?
Nurse 2:	This is befuddling ma!
Sister Kate:	It is very simple: they are husbands to the woman!
Nurse 1:	No! I beg to disagree with you, they are husband!
Nurse 2:	The two of them?
Matron:	Please, enough of this argument. Elder Dominion Akpan has arrived. He has come with fruits, beverages and other assorted food items. I saw him offloading those things from his car when Sister Kate came in to inform me that Alhaji Sule was in the reception. Alhaji must have entered when I went in to the toilet. Can

you imagine a situation that the two of them will meet in this reception as the husbands of the same woman?

Sister Kate: Oh! I see, I was just wondering about what really went wrong... I mean the way you stood up swiftly and brushed me aside on hearing that Alhaji has come...

Matron: You must have thought some strange forces had taken hold of my life?

Sister Kate: Not really... we were just running our minds wide...

Nurse 1: We could not imagine anything concrete...

Nurse 2: We were in a state of thoughtlessness...

Matron: Isn't it unbelievable that your minds were blank? Very unusual. Just unlike being whom I know the three of you to be.

Nurse 1: There had been occasions that we really surprised ourselves ma!

Sister Kate: And, you know that being human at times has no difference from being animals...

Matron: I should know that with my age. Unfortunately, I also occasionally engage in this game of dissimulation...Now, we must be ready. Mr. Dominion Akpan will soon be here. I will go in to my office. Immediately he comes in, you are to usher him into my office.

The Nurses: Okay ma!

Matron: Sister Kate, please, just lead him into my office. We need to manage this case professionally until that woman is more stable and able to recognize her true husband. Is that okay?

The Nurses: Absolutely ma. Perfectly okay ma.

Matron: Good! Let me quickly rush in and settle down. Please, sisters, be professional. No emotions!

The Nurses: Yes Matron!

[*Matron leaves for her office. The nurses try to readjust themselves in readiness to receive Elder Dominion Akpan. Not too long, Elder Dominion Akpan walks in leisurely with an air of self-assurance. He greets them*].

Nurse 1: Our world is full of experiences.

Nurse 2: I am just curious as to how the woman has been able to manage the two men without their knowing each other.

Sister Kate: How are we sure that they don't know each other?

Nurse 2: I easily assume that they don't know each other. You don't really know men. They are proud. They will not agree to be married by any woman as husbands to her at the same time.

Nurse 1: I am dying to find out who the first husband is and who is the second husband? I want to know how they arrange when and who sleeps with the Madam of the house!

Sister Kate: Wonder, they say, shall never end.

[*Elder Dominion Akpan comes in*]

Nurse 1:   Shhhhh, here comes the second husband!

Nurse 2:   Who says he is the second husband? Why can't he be the first husband?

Sister Kate: Stop this argument! Whether he is the first or he is the second, the truth is that the woman has two men laying claim to being her husband! What a lucky woman! Two husband on only her!

Elder D: Good day sisters.

The Nurses: [*Eagerly, with extra ordinary smiles*]. Good day sir. How can we help you sir?

Elder D: Oh, very lovely. I am here to see my wife who is on admission. Her name is Dr. Daniela, PhD Petrochemical Engineering! [*He is full of smile now*] I was also here last night. In fact, I did not leave this place until about 11 pm yesterday.

Nurse 1:   Oh yes, I remember your face now. Sorry for all that happened yesterday... She is in a more stable condition now.

Sister Kate: You are welcome sir. The Matron has requested that we should bring you into her office immediately you arrive.

Nurse 2:   Yes, she did not want you to stay here waiting in a common reception room.

Elder D: Oh, that is very wonderful of her.

Sister Kate: [*Leading the way*]. Please sir, kindly follow me.

Elder D: [*To the two nurses*]. I am very grateful sisters.

The Nurses: It is our pleasure sir.

Elder D: Thank you.

                [*They leave. The nurses cast glances at each other*].

Nurse 2:   Wahala waoooo!

Nurse 1:   Very well, Wahala dey! It reminds me of the song by P-Square [*She picks the song*]

                See me see wahalaeee,

                Wahala dey, wahala dey...

                Oh ohoh, wahala dey...

                As she dey enter... enter,

                Na so some people just dey mental... mental

                Because dem dey feel dis instrumental... mental

                Everybody to the centre... centre

                Omo wahala dey, wahala dey...

Nurse 2:   Wahala waooo, so Christian sister too listens to hip-hop. Do you also do this for special number in church?

Nurse 1:   At times, you get so hazy and careless. And, this is the problem with religious bigots all over the world. So, you expect me to log off my brain and ears anytime I walk down the street or open the television in my house? You seem not to be different from any of your ISIS, Taliban and Bokoharam brothers!

Nurse 2:	*Haba*! *Ki la gbe, ki le ju* [*Haba*, what have I said to warrant such response?]. I don't think we have gone that far...
Nurse 1:	That is how it starts dear. It is when people don't understand how the human mind functions...
Nurse 2:	Well I don't mean it that way. But, you have really said something that sets me thinking just now about ISIS, Taliban and Bokoharam especially in relation to the case on our hands.
Nurse 1:	What? Are you okay? What has ISIS, Taliban and Bokoharam got to do with a woman with two husbands?
Nurse 2:	I am just thinking about any female suicide bomber...
Nurse 1:	Yes, a female suicide bomber and a woman with two husbands, so? What is the relationship?
Nurse 2:	I am just wondering about the hope of female suicide bombers as against the hope of male suicide bombers!
Nurse 1:	Hmmm, hum!
Nurse 2:	A group blow themselves up in the hope of at least seven virgins in heaven, the other group in the hope of nothing!
Nurse 1:	What do you mean by nothing? They would be in the presence of Allah and that should be enough!

Nurse 2: Won't the male suicide bombers be in the presence of Allah with the promised virgins?

Nurse 1: The female suicide bombers will be part of the virgins for the men... they will be given priority, I guess. In everything...the sleeping formula will be in their favour and that should be something dear!

Nurse 2: Women are always schemed out of every narration!

Nurse 1: That is the reason I am in love with this woman. For once, it seems someone is changing the narrativity of women!

Nurse 2: Exactly what I was trying to establish when my mind linked the woman with ISIS, Taliban and Bokoharam. For once, a woman is claiming two men together on earth and not in heaven!

Nurse 1: You mean two men are claiming a woman together on earth and not in heaven!

Nurse 2: *Ijeri aye nijerialikiamo*! [*The witness of earth is the witness of heaven]. So, the two earthly men are claiming her because she is bold to marry them together!

Nurse 1: Well, you know we are not yet sure of the facts of the gist and, I detest unsubstantiated claims. [*In the process of their discussion, a Chinese man walks in agitated. He walks straight to the two nurses*]

Nurse 2: *Ileke ma ja sile ma jasita, ibikanni o jasi* [*To the left or to the right, this story will end somehow!] [*They notice the Chinese man*] Hey, shhhhh, we have a chinchun lee!

Nurse 1: You will always recognize a chinchun lee anywhere!

Chin Chung: Hello sisters!

Nurse 2: [*With extra courtesy*] Hi sir! How can we help you sir?

Chin Chung: Yes, please, I learnt that my wife has been on admission here since two days ago.

Nurses: [*A bit alarmed, they cast glances at each other... as if they are not really sure of what they heard*] Sir! Pardon!

Chin Chung: [*More agitated now*] What! Is she dead? Please, tell me? Please, tell me? I am the husband! Please!

Nurse 1: Who is dead, sir? [*Sister Kate returns. Chin Chung is crying and Kate is confused. She tries to study the situation*]

Nurse 2: We don't seem to understand you sir!

Chin Chung: Please, tell me what has happened to Daniela? Please, tell me what has happened to my wife? I was told she was admitted to this hospital after a ghastly motor accident along Benin-Ore-Sagamu express way two days ago. I am just coming in from Beijing. Please, be sincere with me [*The Nurses are alarmed and confused the more. However, Sister Kate quickly rises to the occasion*]

Sister Kate: Oh sir, please, put yourself together... I guess they have a little challenge with your accent. Daniela, your wife, [*"Your wife" should be emphasized*] is very much in a stable condition. But, please, you will have to follow me to the waiting room while I make arrangement for you to see her as quickly as possible. I assure you sir, she is in a very stable condition.

Chin Chung: [*A little reassured*] Oh, thank you Sister. I am very grateful. That woman means so much to me. She is the centre of my life. Thank you. Please, I can't really wait to see her. Can we go to the waiting room now so that you can speedily arrange my seeing her?

Sister Kate: Right away sir, right away! [*The two exit with Kate leading the way. Nurse 1 and 2 seem perplexed. For about few seconds, they only gaze on the retreating figures with their mouths wide open in total disbelief. They sigh heavily and speak*]

Nurse 1: *Pekelepekele, arugbo je gbese*! [*A very complex matter, the indebtedness of an aged]

Nurse 2: Ta ni o san? [*Who will pay it]

Nurse 1: *Airijinna, lairabuke Okere*! [*If one travels wide, he will likely see a hunched-back squirrel].

Nurse 2: This is now getting extra ordinary. And, if this is true and real, it means that woman is possessed of something outside of this world!

Nurse 1:	Well, people don't get possessed by something within this reality. They get possessed by something outside of this reality...
Nurse 2:	Hmmm! It is getting creepy! [*As if frightened, almost shaking*]
Nurse 1:	Haha, wetin be your own? Hmm, hum, there is no new thing under the heavens! And, as one of my uncles would say, *"Lalaturupus, tululumbus", Lala to lo soke, ile lo mbo*! [*A lala that goes up will surely come down]
Nurse 2:	Hmmm, do you think this is a good omen for this hospital? I am getting scary! An Alhaji, a Yoruba man, an elder, a Calabar man and now, a Chinese man, bringing an international dimension into the story!
Nurse 1:	A story or a tale?
Nurse 2:	What really is the difference?...It is getting spooky for me! Three men, one invalid woman and we don't know if we are just beginning to count!
Nurse 1:	What do you mean by one invalid woman? Are you as valid as that woman? Can you openly marry one and a half men at the same time, not to mention two men? I hate it when people become instantly judgmental when an issue comes to the open like this. We know women who are dating more than seven, eight and nine men together! And, maybe you should search your heart!

Nurse 2: Please, don't bring me into this. I have one man only in my life!

Nurse 1: You mean only one man is openly acknowledged!

Nurse 2: Na you sabi! It is your problem... Look, I hate insinuations! And, what do you even mean? See, if you want us to talk about this freely, I am ready...

Nurse 1: I dare you, *gbogbo eeyan a moohuntaase, tile fi jona* [*everybody will know what we have cooked that sets the house on fire]. Sincerely, if this story is real, it means the woman is daring! Na shego be my first real woman! I mean I will vote her as my First Woman ever!

Nurse 2: *Gba ran mi se wadele rubayiooo* [*How the one helping with a load is transformed to the owner of the load is strange to me]. I don't even know the reason we should be fighting over this matter? What really is our business in it? I am just interested in how this story will end. That is all!

Nurse 1: Sincerely, I wish I could be like this woman the next time I come into this world.

Nurse 2: You are better be mindful of the things you wish for, strange malaikas [*angels] may be passing and if they should sanction your prayers...

Nurse 1: [*Burst into hysteric laughter*] You won't cease to amuse me with your strange beliefs! Just leave me...Sister Kate should come out with the latest and a better gist on this matter *jare*...[*Sister Kate* *replies as if waiting for her to queue her in. She walks in singing another of the P-square songs]*

Sister Kate: [*Singing*] Baba God na your hand work e ee

No be lie e, na your hand work e ee

I say, E no easy ooo, oh ohohohoh,

My brother, my sister, no be today, oh ohohoh

...Na your turn today, another man tomorrow,

My brother wish kind life be dis,

Everybody get his own way to follow,

But e no easy...

...Even if you no get money oh ohoh,

Dey jolly dey shake bodi, ah ahah...

E good oo, e bad ooo, e no easy ohohohohho...

Nurse 1:   Please, Sister Kate, stop this suspense. We are dying to know about how it went over there.

Nurse 2:   Please, Sister Kate, stop this song. P-square will sue you for copyright!

Sister Kate: [*She stops the song*] Now, [*As if thinking seriously*] what has really happened oooo? Friends, nothing! I mean no-thing has happened. Everything remains as they are! One lady patient, three men claiming to be her husbands... all the three men crying their eyes out and dying to see her for the revival of their lost souls!

Nurse 1:   No doubt, their souls must really have been lost! I still don't understand how on earth the woman has been able to manage them. I don't think they really know each other!

Sister Kate: I also don't think so! The woman must be a special evil genius unlike IBB, the self-acclaimed evil genius!

Nurse 2:   Has anyone of them been led to see her today?

Sister Kate: No. Yesterday, while she was still in coma, it was a bit easier to lead the two men to see her separately. But today, she is out of coma. She has started recognising people and the Dr. feels it could have a kind of negative effect on her to be confronted with three men laying claim to her as their wife in a single day. There may be a kind of psychological pressure from a form of stigma or shame that may come with the fact that her secret is probably in the open.

Nurse 1:   Has the Dr. confirmed that the men did not know themselves?

Sister Kate: From all indication, the men are oblivious of the existence of any other man in the life of their wife! Each feel so strongly that he is the only one.

Nurse 2:   So, how come she is one of the three wives of the Alhaji and then a wife to three men, including the Alhaji?

Sister Kate: Well, I am not taking a matriculation examination on this, we are all following this episode together...

Nurse 1:   So, what is going to happen now?

Sister Kate: Matron Haywire has volunteered to speak to her about it.

Nurse 2:   Mama Haywire *niyen* [*That is Mama Haywire for you]. I trust her. That woman is a blessing to this hospital.

Nurse 1:   She is the one who is fit to do such a delicate job. 'Mama Professionalism'... "Look, we must always handle everything professionally without any emotional attachment".

Sister Kate: Sincerely, Matron Haywire is a Strong Breed in her own right!

Nurse 2:   What is it that people like Haywire has not seen?

Nurse 1:   *Oju to tirigelede, tiropiniran* [*The eye that has seen gelede has seen the mother of all show]

Sister Kate: One thing that has just been discovered about the woman is that she is ridiculously rich! In fact, she has requested to be taken to a private ward. Those rooms of half a million naira per day!

Nurse 2:   Whoa!

Nurse 1:   No wonder! It is beginning to make sense now! *Henhen*, I can see the reason three men are dying over her, weeping like babies!

Nurse 2:   That is it!Hmm, *Owo, Ego, Kudi*![*Money!]

Sister Kate:	I have to go now. I have got to leave you chinwags here. [*Jubilant*] I am going to the centre of the revelation.
Nurse 1:	This is the second time you will give it to us raw today! The other time, the accent of that scoundrel was too sophisticated for our comprehension! Now, we are chinwags! No problem. *Ohun to de lonikanwamohun!* [*It is what has come that demands to be known]
Nurse 2:	Forget it, *oni o kiisojoorowa* [*Today is not the day of our banter]
Sister Kate:	[*Hilariously*] So, the two of you could be tamed like this? Wonderful! I now know how to tame you. [*She leaves*].
Nurse 1:	See the way Kate is running her diarrhoea mouth on us because she needs to keep us abreast of the story of this woman!
Nurse 2:	Leave her, it is not her fault. *Iruekuiipedirueeyan* [* No sooner is a rat killed that its tail becomes one's tail]. Are we not the ones who informed her of the story some few hours ago at this very place? The tail of the rat of the story has now become her tail [tale]. Leave her. Today is her day of glory.
Nurse 1:	Let us just forget about her as you have rightly suggested. I am just dying to know how Matron Haywire will open the issue with that woman.
	[*Lights fade slowly on them and come up on a private ward. Sister Kate is by the door. Matron Haywire sits on a seat by the bed of Daniela.*

31

They are engaged in a seeming light discussion about Daniela's life]

Matron: Can I say I am troubled about you! Some strange things ma!

Daniela: Troubled by some strange things about me, Matron? And what are these strange things if I may ask you ma?

Matron: I am actually looking for the most appropriate way to present the issues so as not to embarrass you, you know!

Daniela: Are you trying to speak of my death in parables? See, Matron, don't be afraid to tell me everything about my chances of survival. I have lived my life to the fullest. I am a fan of that promethean, Sisyphus, that absurd hero of men. In fact, I can tell you that I am successfully married to three men [*She laughs heartily*]. I know it will sound very strange to you, but at this stage, I don't have anything to hide again. What I have just told you is only known to my lawyer. I have written my will for the three men and the three children in my life! I have three boys, each for each of the three men in my life!

Matron: [*A bit taken by surprise with her frankness, but unruffled*] I am not totally surprised again. It is actually the knotty issue we have been trying to unravel since yesterday. Yesterday, two men showed up claiming they are your husbands.

Daniela: Oh, I see. Is that what you were looking for the appropriate way to present to me? You are so taken by surprise about its possibility! I could really have sworn that they had been here, except they had not heard of the accident. The two that had come must be Alhaji and Dominion Akpan. They are the Nigerians. I am sure that very shortly Chin Chung will be here from Beijing once he is contacted too.

Sister Kate: He has already come.

Daniela: I could have bet it that once he heard, he would be here. I treated all of them with an unusual feminine charm.

Matron: You are such a strange woman. Look at the way you are talking about what has caused us a lot psychological trauma as if it is not an issue! We were running insane as to how to manage the situation.

Daniela: [*Laughing hysterically*] You must have indeed shared in the burden I have borne for over twenty years now. For twenty two years precisely, after my marriage to Chin Chung, I have had to manage those three men without their knowing each other. I am impressed that you have also managed the three of them in these two days, bravo!

Matron: What! What type of a woman are you? Are you sure of what you are saying?

Daniela: [*With self-assurance*] Madam Matron, do you think I am sounding like a drunk? But even if I sound like one, you know I am not drunk. Well, I may excuse it if you believe that I am under the influence of certain drugs – for I must presume that you have administered certain drugs on me in the last two days. But then, I think I am in a right frame of mind. However, it is possible that you have certain reasons to doubt my humanness that I don't know about?

Matron   You still sound so strange to me...

Daniela: Yes, I will give that to you ma. I must really sound strange against your expectation, against your culture, against your tradition and against your religion...But I know that it is not just about sounding strange; it about being strange to be human!

Matron: You are not disturbed; you are relaxed and comfortable!

Daniela: You missed it, Matron! I was disturbed. I was most uncomfortable. But this accident, this sudden romance with death, it weaned me from my fears. It helped me to realize what would have been after me. It helped me to see through what is important and what is not important. It helped me to realize what it means to be true to oneself. It helped me to realize that we had been a bunch of deception. I am done with that life. It died in the accident!

Matron: Do you think that we have a responsibility to the societal morality?

Daniela: Yes, only women have responsibility to societal morality, men are transcendental. They are free to live above societal morality with the help and the aid of culture, tradition and religion. Matron, we all have responsibility to societal morality. Tell me, what makes men to be different from women in these demands?

Matron: Madam, how do you think these men will react if they realized that they are all at the same time your husbands?

Daniela: Matron, if I may ask you, how do women react when they realize that their husband has more than three or four women in his life as wives?

Matron: I don't know...

Daniela: You only choose not to know Matron. It is always some fretting followed by an uneasy calm!

Matron: Well, now that we know the truth about these men's claims, we will still help you to manage their ignorance.

Daniela: What do you mean Matron?

Matron: We will bring them in to see you separately. I mean one after the other. Each will only have not more than thirty minutes to see you. Hopefully, till you are discharged from here, we would make sure that the ignorance of each exclusivity as your husband is maintained.

Daniela: No! No!! No!!! Matron. I have just told you that the time of ignorance is gone. It is time to bring my husbands together through this time and moment of pain! There is a way this painful accident has to unite us or scatter us forever!

Matron: We are sorry, on behalf of our management, we cannot allow them to know each other here.

Can you imagine the disappointment and the fight that will follow? I am very sure that their tempers will rise beyond your, and our, control. It cannot be a usual sight, no, not at all.

Daniela: Matron, it is not your duty to introduce them to each other, it is my responsibility! I have also not requested that your management should do that, I will. All you need to do is to allow my visitors to see me. Just allow my visitors to see me, I will handle the rest. There's nothing coming from the galaxy that can frighten the earth to flee. We are already at the cross road and we must choose our paths.

Matron: Your choice is a delicate one...

Daniela: It has always been delicately lousy, Matron!

Matron: I would counsel against it. You should still maintain the status quo.

Daniela: Matron, can I ask you a question? But, it may lead to further questions, ma!

Matron: Yes, go ahead. I hope I would be able to answer your questions.

Daniela: Do you practice any religion?

Matron: Yes, I do. I am a Christian.

Daniela: Great! Do you believe in repentance from sin and the doctrine of restitution?

Matron: Yes, I do.

Daniela: But you don't want me to repent and restitute?

Matron: I do like you to repent and restitute, I am only greatly concerned about the circumstances and the timing! Beside, how do you restitute in this type of a situation?

Daniela: You want me to delay my day of salvation? I think repentance is always now and urgent?

Sister Kate: But the issue of this type of restitution is very complex ma!

Daniela: I will simply return to my original owner!

Matron: Your original owner? Among the three men that you had children for? Who is your original owner?

Sister Kate: The first husband, Matron.

Daniela: [*She laughs again*] None of them is my original owner.

Sister Kate: What? Who then is your owner again?

Matron: A fourth man somewhere?

Daniela: Matron! How did you know? I would just have said flesh and blood did not show you that like Jesus.

Sister Kate: Madam! [*Doing a sign of the cross*] Don't add a blasphemy to this issue.

Daniela: You must pity a damned soul? But, I am serious. The Matron is right, I will return to the fourth man in the fiery furnace! I guess we are all owned by God! If nobody accepts me, I will return to him.

Matron:	Hmmm, you are simply an impossible being!
Daniela:	But, the ways of God are not our ways. Salvation is always found in such impossible ways! Well Matron, I have made up my mind. I will receive the three men and introduce them to each other. Don't trouble yourself about the outcome. The dead has nothing to fear again. I am dead!
Matron:	[*Rising*] You are simply impossible! Nothing can describe you, ma!
Daniela:	[*She smiles*] Perhaps your name will do Matron. Look at what you have there on your name tag. I am so fascinated by your name: Haywire! What an inspiration!
Matron:	What?
Sister Kate:	Your name Matron!
Daniela:	It is such an inspiration for what I intend to have now...I see a blue sky out there through the window. I see riotous clouds moving with such unusual swiftness...I look at your name tag, I see Haywire. So, tell me, what could be more inspiring for a woman in the agony of living? Matron, see, I have come a full circle to redefine shame. I will not be a coward again. I am ready to embrace those three men and show them the fourth man! I will be a legend in my own world!
Matron:	In my name, an inspiration? Just as Becket said, there is nothing to be done again!
Sister Kate:	Matron, are you giving up soon?

Matron: At a point, we all will give up.

Daniela: Matron, don't take it to heart too much. Let me tell you, anyhow, we must learn to create fun!

Matron: So, you think you will have fun with three men together?

Daniela: [*She laughs again*] What have I been having all along? I know you think I should be gloomy and sober... You want me to experience the tragic in my story, but I have also learn to see the fools in the great tragedies of Shakespeare! And for my sanity, I have appropriately chosen my character preference. I won't be any of your nobles! Count me out! I will always be a fool. [*Sister Kate discretely leaves*]

Matron: You would not be persuaded?

Daniela: Against my opinion of being a fool, madam? I will end being of the same opinion still, says the sage! It is therefore useless to attempt to persuade any man against his opinion!

Matron: It is okay. We will report to the CMD.

Daniela: My regards Matron.

             [*Lights fade out gradually and rise on the reception. Sister Kate is already with Nurses 1 and 2*].

Sister Kate: He! That woman has signed out completely!

Nurse 2:   Is it out of Yahoo or of Google?

Nurse 1:	No, out of Facebook! Please, this is a serious matter!
Sister Kate:	In all my years, I have never come across an emotionless human being like her!
Nurse 1:	This is serious! You mean she said she wants everything to be "Haywire" in the Matron's name!
Sister Kate:	Not in her name, but as in her name!
Nurse 1:	As chaotic as her name suggests?
Nurse 2:	That the Matron's name is simply an inspiration to her?
Sister Kate:	I have always had a premonition of evil about that name. I mean, how a normal human being can hang such a name tag around her neck: Haywire! Just like the Albatross on the neck of the Ancient Mariner, signifying a curse!
Nurse 1:	But we cannot blame the Matron. She did not give the name to herself!
Sister Kate:	And what parents give their wards such names? Haywire!
Nurse 2:	The Yoruba will say *ilelaawokatosomoloruko*! [*we must consider the events in the home to name a child].
Sister Kate:	*Sho*! So, what was the situation like when the Matron was born?
Nurse 1:	Is that supposed to be a rhetorical question or are we supposed to answer it?

Nurse 2:	The situation could be imagined...But, sincerely, I have always had the temptation to ask the Matron about the inspiration for her name.
Nurse 1:	Same with me. In fact, mine is indeed a struggle!
Sister Kate:	It seems we all had same struggle. But, this temptation, if it is a temptation, is it from the same identified source of eternal temptations: the Devil?
Nurse 2:	You mean we are being tempted on the same thing by the same person? Are you agreeing that there is a devil right there in our minds?
Nurse 1:	I reject it! There is no devil in my heart in Jesus name!
Sister Kate:	She did not mention heart, she said minds!
Nurse 1:	So, where is your mind and where is your heart?
Nurse 2:	Up there in your head, your consciousness!
Sister Kate:	It is okay. The issue will soon degenerate into the theory of the mind and consciousness, but all we are interested in is the inspiration for this haywire situation that made a woman to marry three men together!
Nurse 2:	Thank you Sister Kate, we are almost loosing focus again.
Nurse 1:	One day, I will wean myself of this useless fear; I will ask Matron Haywire about the reason for her name.

Nurse 2:   *Gen gen*! That day, you will definitely experience haywire!

Sister Kate: See, I think the truth is really that we all have our haywire, it is only that we are not favoured to hang it as name tags around our necks!

Nurse 1:   Favoured, how?

Sister Kate: At least, somebody knows that her name is haywire. She knows. She embraces it. She is not feeling funny about it. She has accepted it and she is living with it. But we are ignorant... we feel funny and stupid about it. We are in the bondage of knowing...unfortunately, we are not bold to ask her. We are suffering in the attempt to understand another person's name. We put ourselves in haywire and yet we are blaming the devil!

Nurse 2:   It is okay, I don't want no body to sermonize me...

Nurse 1:   I don't know why we are even like this: we have left the real issue and now, we are fighting and condemning ourselves over frivolous issues!

Sister Kate: We are simply having fun with our haywire moment.

Nurse 1:   Maybe the name is indeed inspiring! [*Matron Haywire rushes in*]

Matron: [*Calling as she comes in*] Kate! Kate!! Kate!!! Kate, what are you doing here at the reception? We have a serious matter on our hands and we must all put our heads together to safe this hospital from this moment of crisis.

Sister Kate:	Exactly what we have been discussing ma. The decision of that woman to have the three men brought together for her utopia idea of repentance and restitution is totally insane. I cannot imagine such irrationality!
Matron:	*O so sinilenu, o buyosi* [*It is a fart rubs with honey comb in one's mouth].
Sister Kate:	The woman thought the issue is just a big joke. Did you see how she was even trying to make a fun of your name, claiming that she is inspired by it? She was not even sensitive to your feelings.
Nurse 1:	Ma, don't you think the accident could have affected a part of her brain – for I don't think that a normal person will claim that she wants to have a moment of haywire?
Nurse 2:	Haywire *ke*?
Matron:	What is wrong with Haywire?
Nurse 2:	The name!
Matron:	What do you mean?
Nurse 1:	It is not your name ma, it is the situation!
Matron:	I see. Anyway, the CMD has met her on the matter. She insisted on her position. So, the CMD has agreed that we should allow her to have it her way. We have alerted and mobilized the Police from Area F.
Nurse 2:	Ha, why Area F? We should have been more sensitive to the "F". It could mean failure. We

should have brought in Police from Areas A, B or C instead!

| Nurse 1: | You have come again with your unproven spirituality! |

| Nurse 2: | I know you are faithless! |

| Nurse 1: | Yes oo, the faith-full! |

| Matron: | Well, sisters, there is no time for a round table on the reason the sewage is dirty! Already, the Police are here. We have taken Alhaji and his two other wives into the ward. I am going in now to take Elder Akpan to meet them. [*Turning to Sister Kate*] Please, Sister Kate, you will take Mr. Chin Chung in right away. At this time, we can only trust that the Lord will save our souls from every form of evil that may arise! |

| The three: | [*Resoundingly with nurse 1 and Kate doing the sign of the Cross*] Amen and amen. Fire! |

[*Matron and Sister Kate exit. Nurses 1 and 2 continue to stare at the retreating figures. Lights fade out gradually but steadily come up on Daniela's ward. Alhaji, Alhaja and Segi are with her*]

| Alhaja: | Subuanala! |

| Segi: | Aunty, I thank God that you are alive. How can we survive as a family without you? |

| Alhaja: | Subuanala!! |

| Alhaji: | She said we should sit down. She said there is a need for a certain serious talk. I only hope that |

all is well Daniela? You are frightening us with this serious talk!

Segi: Aunty, please, please, don't talk about what I am thinking oooo!

Alhaja: Alhaji! She is talking about a serious talk and you are not afraid [*The two women raise a terrible wail*].

Alhaji: What! Daniela! I did not give it such a deep thought! Daniela, how could you...? No! No!! No!!! You are not... you cannot die at this moment!

Daniela: [*With indifference and assurance*] I am not dying. I only want to talk to you about the other men in my life [*Alhaji, Alhaja and Segi stopped in the track of their different displays. Cast unusual glances at each other*]

Alhaji: Daniela, what did you mean?

Daniela: I know you would find it difficult to believe, but I do have two other men in my life with two other sons! [*They are totally distrust and lost*]

Alhaji: Hem, Daniela, if I say I understand what you are saying, I am far from the truth...[*Shouting suddenly*] Matron! Dr! Please, come here. Please, it is urgent!

Daniela: Alhaji, why are you shouting like that?

Alhaji: Oh Daniela! [*Crying*]

Daniela: [*Confused a bit*] Alhaji, why are you crying?

Alhaji: Daniela, please, don't talk too much. You are already stressed up and you need more close medical examination... Please, relax.

Daniela: Oh, I understand...You also think I am out of my mind. Alhaji, I am perfectly in a right frame of mind...I mean...[*Sister Kate leads Chin Chung in to the room*] perfectly...[*Chin Chung ignoring the others moves directly up to Daniela...*]

Chin Chung: Daniela, darling! Oh, I am so sorry. I am so sorry [*He goes to kiss her. Kate stands aside to observe the reaction of others. The others are alarmed and clearly confused the more*] I am happy that you are alive...

Alhaja: Asitani! Sanisatani [*The devil. Separate me from the devil*]. Alhaji, *e n woranni* [*Alhaji, you are just watching*].

Segi: Haram [*A taboo*].

Alhaji: I am lost...I mean totally lost...[*Matron comes in with Elder Dominion Akpan*].

Matron: [*Mischievously*] Elder, here is your wife.

Elder D: [*Moving up to Daniela*] Many thanks Matron. [*Chin Chung is taken aback*]. Daniela, I am happy that you are out of coma. [*He seems to become aware of others*]. Oh, I am very sorry, gentle men and women. Please, pardon me. I was carried away by the eagerness to see my wife. Please, forgive my impulsiveness. [*Matron exchanges glances with Kate. Tension seems heightened now*].

Alhaja: *Subuanala! Sanisatani! Alhaji fa!*

Alhaji: Matron, are you part of this madness? Can somebody tell me what is really happening?

Chin Chung: Please, what is going on in this place?

               [*Matron summons courage to address them*]

Matron: *Hem*, please...excuse me, please...decorum please...We must confess to you that we are as confused as everybody here who desires to understand what is really going on...*Hem*, And, I don't know if your looking at and considering my name tag will be helpful to you in anyway, but if you ever look at it, you will see that my name is haywire! The Madam here, Dr. Daniela, I understand will like to treat us to a situation that is haywire. She has requested that we bring you all into this room for the treat...I think it will be better if we all listen to what she has to say and do.

Elder D: Matron, please, can you be very plain? I don't think I understand the allusion here?

Matron: Elder, there is no allusion here. If you listen to me well, we are all here to listen to your wife tell and explain certain things to us about whatever we do not understand.

Chin Chung: What! His wife or what did you say Matron?

Kate: Yes, his wife, Alhaji's wife and also your wife!

Alhaji: I am double confused! Please, Sister, what are you saying? Nothing is making any sense to me again!

Matron: Nothing about this has really made sense to us either. We are all here to see if we can eventually make a sense of it...

Alhaja: *Subuanala! SaniSatani!*

Segi: [*Singing*]. *Mo re emolereko,*

Ajawewu, o roso,

Eronpilani to mi lo,

Ba mi ki 'ya mi eleko,

Ekomeji re o yo mi, o yo mi oo, o yo mi,

Gbamugbamu, jigijigi, gbamugbamu, jigijigi!

I see a strange sight in Ereko

A dog in Iro and Buba

A plane in the sky

Please, deliver my greetings to my mother, Eleko

That just two of her eko wraps is enough

Gbamugbamu, jigijigi, gbamugbamu, jigijigi!

[*Alhaji in a burst of anger addresses Segi*]

Alhaji: You, what nonsense is that? Is this the time for a useless song? Can you ever be serious for a second! [*Suddenly, he holds his bowels and wriggles with pain*] Yeeee, my stomach! My stomach!! Please, Sister, where is your toilet? Quick before I...

Sister Kate swiftly grabs the hand of Alhaji and pulls him into the toilet]

Sister Kate: Here sir. [*Pushes him in and shuts the door. With a sense of relief*] There would have been a disaster. A bowel eruption right in this place would have dislodged us successfully!

Chin Chung: This is totally silly! Daniela, I demand that you say something here, please!

Elder D: I don't think I am dreaming?...but, this cannot even be a dream...What am I even sure of again? Everything looks foggy somehow! Matron, are we really here with my wife, Daniela...the same woman I visited just yesterday?

Matron: I can be very sure sir! [*Alhaji yells out*]. Take it easy please, Alhaji. Please, softly softly... it could be demanding...

Daniela: Well, I hope all of you will relax and let me address this matter? But then, I want Alhaji to be here to listen to me. However, before he comes out...[*Alhaji cuts in*]

Alhaji: Wait, I am already coming out. I hope it will all just be a strange nightmare and nothing more [*He steps out of the toilet*]...just a strange nightmare with no concrete meaning...

Daniela: Unfortunately Alhaji, this is not a drama! This is a reality. I can agree with the fact that it could be illusionary somehow because you are just being confronted with its facts, but it is real, my dear Alhaji! It is real.

Alhaja: *Subuanala! Sanisatani!*

Matron: Madam, please go on...

Daniela: I am not such a woman who would give useless excuses for what I allowed to happen Alhaji, but you would remember that just three months into our marriage, just three months, I was away on an assignment on the rig in Port-Harcourt and before I returned you had already brought in Alhaja as your second wife! That was thirty years ago!

Alhaji: Yes, I was simply obedient to the injunction of Allah!

Daniela: Just three months into our marriage, Alhaji! You did not even give me any breathing space. If I was not already carrying our baby, I would quit the marriage right then. I held on. And, to safe myself from mental degeneration because of the love you betrayed, I went to start my PhD immediately. I substituted your love for my studies, for books! Immediately I finished my PhD, I requested to be taken back to Port-Harcourt. I made up my mind to marry a second husband, this time around, not as playing any second fiddle role to any man! So, I went for this distrust Akpan. I brought him out of poverty. I spent money on him...

Chin Chung: Holy shit!

Daniela: [*She ignores him*]. I spend money to influence the church to make him an Elder.

Elder D: [*Morose*] Daniela, you made me to ruin me!

Daniela: [*Ignores him*] Alhaji, you will remember that for over two years, I did not come home to see you and my son. I was pumping money to you and Alhaja to take care of my boy. I was pregnant and had another baby boy then. I opened a big electronic shop for Akpan. He became an instant authority in town and in the church! By that time, you took your third wife, Segi. Technically, by then you were no longer really married to me but to my money and wealth! Whenever I come home to see my boy, you would plead with me to be given another chance to show what you normally called your true love to me again.

Alhaja: *Subuanala!* Alhaji, is that true? But that is not what you normally tell us about her!

Segi: Ha, I have suffered! You were begging her, you were beating us!

Alhaji: Keep quiet about what you know nothing about, fools! Where did you think I was getting all the money from? Who did you think paid for your pilgrimage to Mecca? But, Daniela...

Daniela: Alhaji, will you please allow me to finish this story...

Chin Chung: Holy shit! You are very mad Daniela! You have ruined my life and that of our boy...I thought I have a wife, a son and a home, but now...I am just one of the three husbands in your life and our son is just one of your three sons...You are mad.

Elder D: Indeed, our wife has gone mad!

Alhaji: Can you listen to yourself, [mimicking] "Our wife has gone mad", should people outside there hear this nonsense, that three of us are married to...what am I even saying, that three of us are married by a woman?

Chin Chung: Holy shit! This is ridiculous...I am messed up. I cannot continue to listen to this shit! [*He storms out of the room*]

Kate: The Chinese is gone, madam, but you have not explained how you met him?

Daniela: Leave him, he is now a man. I picked him from a ghetto in Beijing. I polished his life up. He is now a man...Let him go with pregnancy and return to me with a baby! It was when I went to Beijing for an international exchange programme in relation to oil and gas exploration. I decided that I was going to march Alhaji's number. I went for him and we had a baby boy...

Matron: You did all this because of Alhaji?

Daniela: No! Not really because of him. I did it because of myself. I did it because of our culture. I did it to rewrite the traditions. I did it to make significant contribution to our way of life. I did it to deconstruct and reconstruct reality. In any case, what really is a reality out of what you see or perceive?

Alhaja: *Segi, koju ma ribi...* [*Segi, if our eyes will see no evil...*]

Segi: Alhaja, *gbogbo araloogun e* [*Alhaja, the whole body is its antidote]

Alhaja: Alhaji, it is a disaster to be married to a man who is not a man. We are going. If we are still at home when you return, we will hear how it is resolved [*Alhaja and Segi exit*].

Alhaji: Daniela, you have ruined my life. You have ruined my home. See how I am losing everything...

Daniela: At times, we have to lose everything to really find ourselves and our purpose, Alhaji. Do you really think it is bad to lose everything to find ourselves?

Alhaji: Daniela you are indeed mad! You are insane. I regret ever coming in contact with you. You are the Asitani [*Satan] that should be stoned to death! [*He makes attempt to attack her but for the quick intervention of Matron and Kate*]. If I have a cutlass I would have shown you instant sharia! You deserve to die...

Daniela: [*She laughs heartily*] Alhaji, don't tell me your stoning of Asitan in Mecca was a waste of energy, time and resources? You mean I spent that money on your pilgrimage to Mecca for nothing! [*Alhaji struggles to free himself from Matron and Kate*]

Alhaji: Leave me Matron! Leave me and let me deal with this useless whore!

Matron: We are very sorry Alhaji. She is your wife. When she is discharged from here, you will have the time and the space to deal with her appropriately.

Alhaji: This prostitute is not my wife again! It may take long but don't be fooled to think you will escape my sharia [*He storms out of the room*]

Daniela: He is not a whore since his actions are sanctioned by Allah. I am a whore because I carried out my own decisions and desires...and invented my own culture. Matron, thank you for restraining the animal!

Sister Kate: Elder Akpan, you are the only one left with her.

Elder D: No, I am not with her...I am not even with myself. I am ruined. How do I explain this to the church leadership? How do I tell all the elders of my village...? How do I tell our son...that our wife...oh! Rubbish...that my wife has gone mad? [*He sobs as he walks away. Matron and Kate look at each other. Daniela sigh heavily. It is silent a while, then Matron speaks*]

Matron: They are all gone madam!

Daniela: Yes, you think they are all gone... but, they are in the web, they have only temporarily moved to a part of it. We are all caught in the web of living and having our haywire experiences. Some will choose to enjoy it, some will choose to rupture it and some will choose to destroy it [*The two Nurses at the reception rush in panting*]

Matron: What is the matter with you?

Nurse 1: We saw them leaving...

Nurse 2:   We were afraid something strange had happened to you...

Nurse 1:   We decided to come and confirm for ourselves...

Sister Kate: We are here.

Matron: Nothing unexpected has happened.

Nurses 1&2:   Really! They all took it in good faith? That is strange!

Sister Kate: Madam, what will you do now?

Daniela: I will do nothing than meet the fourth man!

Nurse 1&2:   What? A fourth man again!

Matron and Sister Kate: [*They look at Daniela with a smile*]. Don't mind these gossips; they are strangers to your world!

Blackout!

[*Wahala dey begins to play*]

House lights